W9-BFF-003

AN INTERACTIVE MODERN HISTORY ADVENTURE

by Michael Burgan

Consultant:
Raymond L. Puffer, PhD
Historian, Ret.,
Edwards Air Force Base History Office

CAPSTONE PRESS
a capstone imprint

Choose Books are published by Capstone Press,
) Roe Crest Drive, North Mankato, Minnesota 56003
v.capstonepub.com

Library of Congress Cataloging-in-Publication Data
Burgan, Michael.
  The Korean War : an interactive modern history adventure / by Michael Burgan.
    pages cm. — (You choose. Modern history)
  Summary: "Lets readers experience the Korean War from multiple perspectives,
allowing them to choose different paths through history"— Provided by publisher.
  Includes bibliographical references and index.
  ISBN 978-1-4914-0355-6 (library binding)
  ISBN 978-1-4914-0357-0 (paperback)
  ISBN 978-1-4914-0359-4 (ebook PDF)
1. Korean War, 1950–1953—Juvenile literature. 2. Korea (South)—Juvenile literature.
3. Korea (North)—Juvenile literature. 4. Korea—History—Juvenile literature. I. Title.
  DS918.B862 2015
  951.904'2—dc23   2014013067

Editorial Credits
Mandy Robbins, editor; Bobbie Nuytten, designer; Wanda Winch, media researcher;
Charmaine Whitman, production specialist

Photo Credits
AP Images, 12, 33, Korea News Service/Korean Central News Agency, 27; Capstone,
9; Corbis: Bettmann, 10, 83, N.H. McMasters, 17; Criaimages.com: Jay Robert Nash
Collection, 21; Getty Images: AFP, 78, Central Press, 70, 102, Gamma/Keystone,
86, Interim Archives, 40, 47; Keystone, 25, 63, Time & Life Pictures/Hank Walker,
38, UIG/Sovfoto, 55, 56; National Archives and Records Administration, 6, 75;
Shutterstock: cluckva, grunge wall, leungchopan, jungle vegetation; U.S. Army/Feldman,
66, Peterson, cover, Pfc. Donald Dunbar, 49, Pfc. Tom Nebbia, 95; U.S. Marine Corps/
Cpl. McDonald, 81; U.S. Navy/C.K. Rose, 93

Printed in Canada.
032014   008086FRF14

TABLE OF CONTENTS

4

ABOUT YOUR ADVENTURE

YOU are living in 1950, when North Korea shocks the world by invading South Korea. The United States sends troops to help South Korea. How will you be involved in the coming war?

In this book you'll explore how the choices people made meant the difference between life and death. The events you'll experience really happened.

Chapter One sets the scene. Then you choose which path to read. Follow the directions at the bottom of each page. The choices you make will change your outcome. After you finish one path, go back and read the others for new perspectives and more adventures.

YOU CHOOSE the path
you take through history.

United Nations troops crossing the 38th parallel, which split North and South Korea

Invasion in Korea

Like many people, you're stunned when North Korea invades South Korea on June 25, 1950. The two countries were once a joint independent nation. But in 1910 Korea came under Japanese rule.

Japan ruled harshly until the United States and its allies defeated the Japanese in 1945, ending World War II (1939–1945). The Allies included the Soviet Union, which has since split into Russia and 14 other countries. After the war Soviet troops held the northern part of the Korean peninsula, while American troops controlled the south. The 38th north parallel of latitude split the two regions.

Turn the page.

The Soviets and the Americans didn't trust each other. Americans believed Soviet leader Joseph Stalin wanted to spread Soviet communism around the world. Under communism, one political party controls the government, which owns most property and businesses. U.S. leaders saw communism as a threat to the world's political and economic freedom.

After World War II, the United States and Soviet Union entered what was called the Cold War. Each side wanted to spread its form of government to other countries. Each wanted to stop the other from gaining more influence in world affairs. The war was "cold" because the two countries didn't fight each other. Instead each nation helped other countries in their wars. The first "hot" war of the era came in Korea.

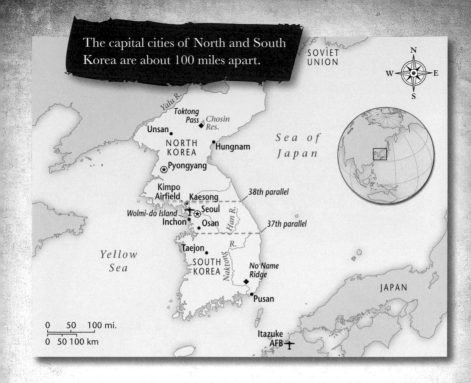

The capital cities of North and South Korea are about 100 miles apart.

Communist leader Kim Il Sung and his allies took control of northern Korea. Syngman Rhee was the top political leader in the south. He strongly opposed communism. In 1948 Rhee won the first presidential election in the newly independent Korea. But the northern Koreans rejected the election and Rhee's victory. Kim and the communists then formed their own government.

9

Turn the page.

Syngman Rhee, who was president of South Korea from 1948 to 1960, displays the Korean flag.

Kim wanted to reunite the country under his rule. That desire led to North Korea's surprise attack on the south. Kim convinced Joseph Stalin to support the invasion. Another communist nation, China, also backed it. The United States supported South Korea. The United Nations (UN) also agreed to help the south, and 15 nations eventually sent troops to Korea.

You hoped World War II would be the last major war. But now war will once again affect millions of people, including you.

To be a pilot in the U.S. Marines, turn to page **13**.

To be an American who volunteers to fight, turn to page **39**.

To be a South Korean civilian at the start of the war, turn to page **71**.

U.S. Marines board a Navy transport vessel in San Diego, California, bound for Korea.

CHAPTER 2

Flying Over Korea

You're living in Chicago when North Korea invades the south. You served as a Marine pilot during World War II. When the war ended, you joined the Marine Corps Reserve. You have continued to receive training.

Because of the invasion, the military needs as many soldiers as possible to fight in Korea. You receive orders to leave for the Marine aviation base at El Toro, California. You say good-bye to your wife, Mary, and your children, Karen and Joey.

13

After a long train ride, you reach the Marine base in California. The Marines still use the fighter plane you flew in World War II, the F4U Corsair. It can drop bombs or fire guns at enemies on the ground while battling other planes in the air.

Turn the page.

The Marines also fly helicopters. The Korean War is the first time helicopters will be widely used in combat. They'll carry officers to the front lines and take wounded troops to Mobile Army Surgical Hospital (MASH) units.

At El Toro you meet your commanding officer, Colonel Jonathan Harrison. He says, "I see you've flown Corsairs. We need experienced pilots to learn to fly helicopters too. Are you interested?"

You know the Corsair well. But it might be interesting to fly helicopters, even though they are more dangerous to fly than planes.

14

To fly a helicopter, go to page **15**.

To fly a Corsair, turn to page **20**.

You quickly learn how important helicopters will be in the war. Korea's many mountains and poor roads make traveling difficult. Helicopters can move men and supplies where trucks and airplanes can't.

As you train you hear news of the fighting. The communists won many early victories in the south, but South Korea's Republic of Korea (ROK) Army and the first U.S. troops stopped their advance near Pusan. Marines next carried out a successful amphibious invasion at the port of Inchon. That battle drove North Korean troops far back north into their own country.

15

Turn the page.

As U.S. troops approached the North Korean/Chinese border, hundreds of thousands of Chinese troops suddenly entered the battle against the American and UN forces. The Chinese pushed the UN troops south of the 38th parallel.

As 1951 begins many Americans are fighting a force of mostly Chinese troops in areas near the 38th parallel. You leave for Korea in early January 1951. You're with the 1st Marine Division, which is fighting outside Seoul. Pilots in this division fly two types of helicopters. One is the Sikorsky HO3S. The other is the Bell HTL. It's similar to helicopters you trained on at El Toro. The Marines often use it to take wounded soldiers to MASH units. Your new commander, Colonel Earl Morris, asks which one you'd like to fly.

Each chopper has its disadvantages. Pilots sometimes have to load the Sikorsky with bags of sand to keep it balanced in flight. But the Bell can have engine problems and carries less fuel, so it can't fly as far.

To fly the Sikorsky, turn to page **18**.

To fly the Bell, turn to page **31**.

Wounded Marines are evacuated to a MASH unit in a Sikorsky helicoper.

You tell Morris you'd like to fly the Sikorsky. "You'll see plenty of action," he says. "General Ridgway has ordered a new offensive."

Matthew Ridgway commands the 8th U.S. Army. Your Marine division is under his control. He wants to force Chinese troops still in South Korea back across the 38th parallel. The first part of the attack is called Operation Killer.

As U.S. forces fight on the ground, you carry out missions in the skies. At times you provide information about the roads and terrain ahead of the troops. Your findings help commanders know where to send troops.

As the fighting increases in March 1951, you receive an order to fly behind enemy lines. "The Chinese shot down a U.S. Air Force plane," Morris explains. "We want you to find it and rescue anyone who survived."

This is a dangerous mission. The Sikorsky doesn't carry any weapons. The only defense you have is the rifle carried by your mechanic, Sergeant Bobby Pulaski.

You fly over the rugged mountains and frozen rivers. You see where bombing has blackened the land. Then you spot something to your left.

Two crew members from the downed Air Force plane stand by the wreckage. You start to go down when you hear the sound of metal hitting metal. Someone is firing at you!

"The Chinese are down there!" Bobby shouts. "Maybe we should radio for help."

19

To call for help, turn to page **29**.

To keep going, turn to page **30**.

You begin training again with a Corsair, and in September you sail to Japan. The war has gone badly so far for the Americans and their allies. But they've managed to stop the North Koreans at Pusan. General Douglas MacArthur is planning a huge amphibious assault. The target is the port city of Inchon on the Yellow Sea.

The first attacks come September 13. You fly your Corsair off an aircraft carrier. You and other Marine pilots attack the small island of Wolmi-do in the harbor. Some of the planes carry napalm, a chemical that burns almost anything it touches. Your Corsair carries rockets.

As the attack begins, you fly low over the island. You fire your rockets at North Korean military trucks. Some of them try to escape, but you swoop down just above the streets. An enemy truck bursts into flames as one of your rockets hits it.

Corsairs fly in formation on their way to support ground troops.

Turn the page.

The ground assault follows September 15. The Marines and ROK troops quickly control Inchon. MacArthur's plan is a success, and now the Americans will push the North Koreans far back to their own country.

Before that happens your commander, Colonel Clarence Scott, approaches you.

"The Marines are getting some jets," he says. "Would you like to learn to fly one?"

It would be exciting to try something new. But flying a plane you don't know well in combat could be dangerous.

To continue flying a Corsair, go to page **23**.

To fly a jet, turn to page **26**.

"Sir, I'd prefer to stick with a plane I know." Scott nods and tells you to be ready for more missions.

The war goes better for the UN forces as they capture the North Korean capital of Pyongyang. But in late October, China sends hundreds of thousands of troops to help the North Koreans. They drive the Americans and their allies back south.

By late November the Marines you support are stuck at Chosin Reservoir, in the middle of North Korea. Chinese forces have closed in on three sides as temperatures plunge to 30 degrees below zero. If you touch the metal on your Corsair, your skin sticks to it.

Turn the page.

U.S. troops have to fight their way out to reach safety. The "Chosin Breakout" takes almost two weeks. You and the other pilots take shifts, so planes are in the air almost around the clock.

As the breakout goes on, you are exhausted from flying so much. One day you drop napalm bombs to help Marines under attack. You release one bomb and then another. But the second bomb falls too soon. You're horrified to realize that the chemical will hit some of your own troops. You radio another pilot, Lieutenant Archie Johnson, and tell him what happened.

24

"You can't think about that now," Johnson says. "If you can't handle the pressure, maybe you should go back to the base."

U.S. ground troops in Korea under attack from enemy fire

You don't want to make any more mistakes.

But the Marines below are still under attack.

You can fire your machine guns to help them.

To return to base, turn to page **32**.

To keep attacking, turn to page **34**.

You're training on an F9F Panther. Its top speed is 545 miles per hour, more than 100 miles per hour faster than the Corsair. As in your other missions, you'll be called to help Marines on the ground. You'll also attack targets in North Korea, such as trucks and trains carrying supplies to the enemy.

You will face enemy fighter planes as well. China entered the war in October 1950 to help North Korea. Chinese pilots fly MiG-15 fighters built in the Soviet Union.

Once you're trained, you fly dozens of attack missions. You battle MiGs in some of the first dogfights ever between two jets.

Chinese pilots flew Soviet MiGs during the Korean War.

In one dogfight a group of MiGs flies above the slower Panthers. Then they come back around to attack you from behind. You bank your plane hard to the right. Then you make a turn that puts you behind one of the MiGs. You fire your machine guns. Black smoke trails from the enemy plane's tail.

"I got one!" you radio back to base. It's the fourth MiG you've shot in your Panther. The other enemy planes fly off.

27

Turn the page.

Colonel Scott visits you when you return to the base. "You did a good job today," he says. "One more and you'll be an ace." An ace is a pilot who shoots down five or more enemy planes.

"And I'm ready to get that fifth," you say with a smile. Then the colonel reminds you that your tour of duty is almost over.

"You can extend the tour," he says. "But I know you have a family waiting for you."

You miss Mary and the kids. But you would love to become an ace—not many pilots have the skill to do it.

28

To sign up for another tour of duty, turn to page **35**.

To go home, turn to page **37**.

You call for help before turning back toward the base. As the Sikorsky turns, several bullets shatter the rotor. The helicopter dives. You frantically move the joystick, but nothing happens. As rocky ground gets closer, you close your eyes and wait for the crash.

The Sikorsky lands hard, then rolls over. Strapped into your seat, you think you're OK.

"Bobby?" you call. But he doesn't respond. The crash has knocked him out—or worse. Now you can only hope to be rescued before the Chinese find you.

29

THE END

To follow another path, turn to page 11.
To read the conclusion, turn to page 103.

"I'm going down there," you say. "These choppers can take a lot of hits."

A few more enemy bullets pierce the chopper, but you're able to land next to the plane. The two airmen scramble in, and you take off. The chopper has only two seats, so the rescued men cling to the doorway. To avoid the enemy, you take a different flight path. But it's getting dark, and the Sikorsky isn't equipped to fly at night. You radio the base. As you approach, you see trucks and jeeps on the field with their lights on. With their help you safely land the chopper.

"Nice work," Colonel Morris tells you. But you know you're lucky to have made it back alive.

THE END

To follow another path, turn to page 11.
To read the conclusion, turn to page 103.

To carry wounded Marines, the Bell has a litter on each of the skids it uses to land. The wounded men are strapped into the litters. You perform some missions at night, even though the Bell isn't designed for night flight. These missions are especially dangerous, but if you don't fly, soldiers could die.

As the fighting goes on, you pick up more wounded men than you can count. Inside the MASH unit, you sometimes even help out in the operating room.

After a year in Korea, you return to the United States. You're happy to see Mary and the kids again. But you know you will never forget the faces of the dead and wounded Marines who fought bravely for their country.

THE END

To follow another path, turn to page 11.
To read the conclusion, turn to page 103.

You pull off from Johnson and the other Corsairs and head back to the base. But as you do, a radio report comes in about Marines trapped by enemy artillery. You take the Corsair to almost full speed and then see the Marines on a hill. To the west are puffs of smoke from the Chinese guns. You dive down, firing all your machine guns. As you pull up, you hear bullets hitting your plane.

You push the Corsair to fly even faster, but you can't get away. Chinese bullets pelt your engine. The plane starts to plunge into a steep hillside. Just before you crash, you think that at least you did all you could to help your fellow Marines.

THE END

To follow another path, turn to page 11.
To read the conclusion, turn to page 103.

32

Members of the First Marine Brigade make their way to the front lines.

33

"We've got a job to do," you tell Johnson. "Come on!"

You swing around to attack the Chinese positions. As you start to descend, your engine sputters. Gunfire must have hit the plane. Your only hope is to jump out before the plane crashes. You quickly pull open the canopy.

You slide onto the top of the wing and jump. Your parachute opens as it should. As you drift down, you wonder who will find you first, the Americans or the Chinese. You see a group of soldiers standing in a circle, their rifles pointed skyward. By their puffy winter coats, you know they're Chinese. As you hit the ground, they surround you. You know your next stop will be a prisoner of war camp.

34

THE END

To follow another path, turn to page 11.
To read the conclusion, turn to page 103.

"I'm staying, sir," you tell the colonel. He seems surprised, but takes you into his office to fill out the paperwork.

It's now late 1952. The war drags on, even as neither side gains much ground. You fly more missions but never spot enemy planes. But that changes one day on a mission to destroy Chinese supplies. You see a lone MiG.

"This one is mine," you radio the other pilots.

Since the MiG flies so much faster than your Panther, it could easily escape. But the Chinese pilot circles back to fight you.

35

You blast away with your machine guns and see flames erupt from the MiG's engine. He's done! The pilot ejects from the plane and floats into the mountains below.

Turn the page.

Back at base other pilots congratulate you on becoming an ace. One of them is new, but his face looks familiar. He shakes your hand.

"Great job," he says. "I'm Ted Williams."

Ted Williams is one of the greatest hitters ever in baseball! Like you, he was a Marine pilot during World War II. Now he's flying again.

"Mr. Williams," you stammer, "you're one of my heroes."

He shakes his head. "You're the hero, kid, for serving your country so well."

36

THE END

To follow another path, turn to page 11.
To read the conclusion, turn to page 103.

"It's more important to see my kids than to get that fifth plane," you say. You board a transport plane that will take you from South Korea to Japan. From there, you'll sail home.

The weather is gray and rainy when you leave Korea. Wind bounces the plane around. Suddenly you hear a loud noise. The plane turns back toward the base.

A storm is brewing as the plane approaches the airfield. Lightning flashes around the plane. The transport dives toward the ground—too fast. It's going to crash!

37

You brace for the collision. When it comes, part of the plane breaks in two. Amazingly, all on board survive. Tomorrow you'll get to go home.

THE END

To follow another path, turn to page 11.
To read the conclusion, turn to page 103.

U.S. soldiers advance toward the capital of North Korea.

CHAPTER 3

Choosing to Fight

It's 1949 and you're eager to join the military. At 16 you can choose to leave school. You plan to enlist. Your parents don't like the idea.

"You're too young," your father says. "You have to be 17 to enlist—and then you need our permission."

"I can lie about my age," you say. "My friend Jim did it to join the Marines."

Dad shrugs his shoulders. "Well, since your mind is made up, go ahead and try."

39

Your 18-year-old cousin Harry wants to enlist too. You both decide to join the reserves. Then you can hold a job and get military training at the same time. You'll be a full-time soldier only if the country goes to war.

Turn the page.

An Army infantry machine gun crew is ready to face the enemy.

You and Harry are not sure which military branch to join.

"The Marines are the toughest fighters," Harry says. "Look at how well they did against the Japanese during World War II."

"But the Army is just as important," you say. "Plenty of soldiers fought well in Europe."

Harry replies, "Well, they're both good. You decide which we should join."

To join the Marines, go to page **41**.

To join the Army, turn to page **48**.

You and Harry head to the local Marine recruiting office. When the sergeant asks your age, you say, "I'm 17, sir."

You're tall and muscular, so he doesn't question you. He explains that you'll attend a session every week to learn the basics of being a Marine. During the summer you'll go to a two-week camp to learn more skills. You take the enlistment forms to your father, who reluctantly signs them.

The weekly drills and the summer training camp are not too hard. You like that you're learning something about the Marines while still earning money at a local factory.

41

Turn the page.

As June 1950 begins, you're thinking about your second summer training session. But before you go, North Korea invades South Korea. You and Harry receive the news that reservists will now be full-time Marines. And many of you will be going to Korea.

You travel to the Marine base at Fort Pendleton in California. A sergeant looks over the training you've had. "I think you need more training before you can fight," he says. "But you have a choice. Do you think you're ready for combat?"

To get more training, go to page **43**.

To skip more training, turn to page **62**.

You and Harry both tell the sergeant you want to stay for more training. But even that won't be as much as a regular Marine would get. The Marines need you in Korea as soon as possible.

You and Harry are assigned to different companies. You say good-bye, knowing you may never see each other again. You sail from California to Japan, your first stop. Your training continues on the ship with Marines who fought during World War II. You're now a lance corporal and will be firing a machine gun. Another Marine, Private Rocky Stern, will carry ammunition for you and other gunners.

43

Turn the page.

When you reach South Korea, the Americans and their allies have already pushed the North Koreans back across the 38th parallel. The fighting goes well there until the Chinese enter the war in October to help North Korea.

One late November night, you and the rest of your company crawl into the foxholes you've dug. You tighten your sleeping bag around you. The temperature plunges to 20 below zero. You haven't shaved for days, and ice clings to your beard. You and Rocky sleep back to back, so you can see around you in case of an enemy attack. Suddenly you hear the sound of bugles mixed with the yells of thousands of men. The Chinese are attacking!

You and Rocky scramble from your sleeping bags and head for the machine gun.

Sergeant Charlie Rizzo, who leads the machine gun squad, wakes the other men.

You set up your machine gun and start firing. The bullets cut down the first advancing Chinese, but more rush forward.

"We have to pull back," Rocky says. "There are too many of them."

You look for Rizzo. But the sergeant is on the ground and not moving. You think he's dead.

Other Marines around you are holding their ground. But some are pulling back, without waiting for an order.

45

To keep fighting, turn to page **46**.

To retreat, turn to page **68**.

You jump out of your foxhole, grasping your machine gun. Rocky quickly finds another gun near a dead Marine. You run for some large rocks beyond your camp. You hear bullets bouncing off the rocks.

You and Rocky find a tight spot in the rocks. It's just wide enough for you to inch in and take cover. For several minutes you hear the sounds of battle. Mortar shells and grenades explode. Then you hear the sounds of planes followed by the rapid fire of their machine guns.

When the battle noises finally stop, Rocky
46 moves out first. You walk past the bodies of dead and wounded men. Your machine gun sits on a tripod and is too heavy to fire on the run. You find a dead Marine and take his rifle and grenades.

As you approach a foxhole, you hear several men talking in an unfamiliar language. They must be Chinese soldiers. "We should check it out," you whisper.

"There could be a lot of them," Rocky says. "Let's keep going."

To investigate the foxhole, turn to page **65**.

To pass it, turn to page **67**.

47

Two Marines remain on guard in their foxhole.

You and Harry go to the Army recruiting office. The sergeant there doesn't look twice when you say you're 17. You're surprised that some of your military education will be through courses you take by mail. You'll also have about two weeks of real training each summer.

"There's not enough money for much real training," the sergeant explains. "If you're lucky, you'll train with soldiers who fought during World War II."

When your training time comes, you do meet veterans from the last war. They teach you to fire a rifle and how to stay alive on a battlefield.

In June 1950 you hear that North Korea has invaded South Korea. The United States is going to war again. In July the government asks for volunteers from the reserves to go on active duty. Harry says he's going to volunteer. You're not sure.

To volunteer, turn to page **50**.

To stay home, turn to page **52**.

Soldiers in the Korean War had to be resourceful, even cooking meals in their foxholes.

During your last round of training, you learn to fire a Browning automatic rifle (BAR). It fires 550 rounds of ammunition per minute. Your platoon leader, Sergeant Mac Richards, makes sure you get a BAR when orders come for you to go to Korea.

In San Francisco, California, you board a ship for Korea. You come ashore at the city of Pusan and take a train to the city of Taegu. Your platoon moves out into the countryside, where the North Koreans hold several hills. You slog through muddy rice paddies. When you reach dry land, you set up an outpost ahead of the main company of soldiers. You and the other men dig foxholes about four feet deep and try to get some sleep.

Just after midnight you awake to the sound of mortar fire. The North Koreans are attacking! You peer out of your foxhole. About 150 enemy troops approach in the moonlight.

"We're going to charge them," Richards says. "Fix your bayonets!"

Your BAR doesn't have a bayonet. Should you stay in the foxhole? But you could still fire the rifle.

51

To stay in the foxhole, turn to page **58**.

To charge the enemy, turn to page **59**.

You tell Harry you're going to wait for the government to call you. The next month you get orders to report for training at Fort Dix in New Jersey. During training you make a friend, Sam Jones. You learn about American successes at Inchon, as well as the terrible defeats after China enters the war in October 1950.

In January 1951 you and Sam join an Army unit based near Pusan, South Korea. Sergeant Ralph Schmidt tells you about the fierce fighting the unit faced around the Chosin Reservoir. "When November started, we were ready to take all of North Korea—or so we thought. The Chinese forced us back behind the 38th parallel."

By the end of January, your unit is on the move. Your goal is to force the Chinese out of mountains not far from Seoul. Marching in the cold, wet weather takes a toll on your feet. Some soldiers get trench foot. The skin on their feet becomes blistered and infected and sometimes falls off.

With Sergeant Schmidt leading the way, you're sent to scout the Chinese positions. If they see you and fire, you can call in artillery strikes against them. One night a group of Chinese soldiers sneaks up on your company. As they fire on the guards, you and the other scouts scramble from your foxholes to fire back. But seeing you're outnumbered, you retreat.

53

Turn the page.

Heading back to camp, you feel a hot, piercing pain in your leg. You've been shot! You fall to the ground, screaming. Two soldiers pick you up, but they are cut down by Chinese machine guns. You play dead, hoping the Chinese soldiers will leave you alone. But one touches your wounded leg with his gun. You twitch. The Chinese drag you to a small group of American prisoners. One of them is your buddy, Sam. You inch over to him.

He whispers, "We should run for it."

"You're crazy," you say. "They'll kill us."

"I'd rather die trying to escape than get sent to a POW camp," Sam says grimly.

54

To try to escape, go to page **55**.

To stay with the other prisoners, turn to page **60**

A group of U.S. prisoners of war (POWs) marches to a Korean prison camp.

"OK," you say. The Chinese force you to 55 march north. With each step, your leg throbs, but you try to ignore the pain. That night you hear rifle shots and whistles. Your guards force you into nearby ditches. Soon you see why. American bomber planes are flying overhead.

Turn the page.

After the planes leave, the Chinese begin to move again. The other prisoners climb out of the ditch. But what if you and Sam just stayed in yours? It's so dark that the guards might not notice you. You crouch even lower into the hole. You hear the sound of marching footsteps and Chinese voices fading away. It worked!

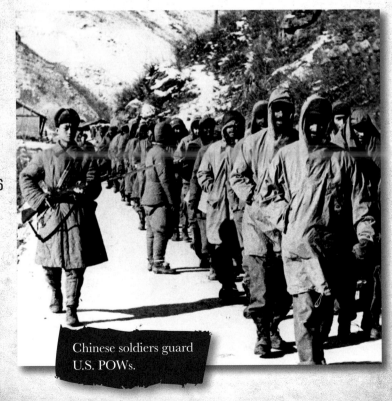

Chinese soldiers guard U.S. POWs.

You wait several more minutes to make sure the Chinese are gone. Then you and Sam jump out of the ditch and begin walking in the opposite direction.

As morning comes you see a farmer working in a rice paddy. You can't speak each other's language, but he understands that you're lost. He points south—that must be where the Americans are. As you walk in that direction, you hear a buzz overhead. It's an American plane! The pilot can't land, but he'll radio for someone to come get you and Sam.

THE END

To follow another path, turn to page 11.
To read the conclusion, turn to page 103.

It's safer to stay in the foxhole. You see many fellow soldiers killed by enemy fire. One of them is Sergeant Richards. The surviving men drive off the North Koreans, but you are horrified by what you see. You begin to cry uncontrollably.

An officer from the main company pulls you out of the hole. He asks your name, but you can't speak. The officer calls over a medic.

"Get him out of here," the officer says. "We don't need soldiers who can't take battle."

The medic comforts you as he leads you away. "It's OK," he says. "A lot of guys can't handle the killing. We'll send you to Japan for some rest."

58

You hear the shots and screams of battle as you leave. You hope to never hear them again.

THE END

To follow another path, turn to page 11.
To read the conclusion, turn to page 103.

You charge out, firing your BAR as you run. Richards and the others reach the main body of North Koreans. You watch with amazement as several grenades bounce off Richards before they explode. He stumbles but keeps running. You manage to catch up to him and the others.

Finally the two forces meet in hand-to-hand combat. You swing your rifle butt at a North Korean and knock him down. But as you turn, a bayonet from another North Korean pierces your chest. As you fall to the ground, dying, you know you've chosen to fight bravely.

59

THE END

To follow another path, turn to page 11.
To read the conclusion, turn to page 103.

The march to the POW camp takes several weeks. Your leg hurts, but you force yourself to keep walking. You find a stick to use as a crutch. The Chinese kill soldiers who are too wounded to walk.

Finally you reach a camp near North Korea's border with China. You and dozens of other men are forced into a small wooden building with no heat. The food is awful—just handfuls of wormy corn. It's barely enough to keep you alive, and your leg is still sore. Somehow you didn't get an infection, but the bullet is still inside.

60

One prisoner tries to help you and others. His name is Captain Emil Kapuan, and he is a Catholic priest serving as a military chaplain. Kapuan searches for extra food for the sickest men.

The Chinese give the prisoners lessons about Communism. They teach them that Communism is the best system and the United States is weak.

"Don't listen to them," Kapuan says. "Would Americans treat our prisoners like this?"

Kapuan is thin and weak. One of his legs is swollen and black from a blood clot. The Chinese take him to a hospital, but it has no doctors. They just want him to die alone.

In May you learn the chaplain is dead. You decide that if you survive, you'll tell others about this brave man. In September 1953 you are released. Your eyes fill with tears as you realize you'll soon be going home.

61

THE END

To follow another path, turn to page 11.
To read the conclusion, turn to page 103.

You're assigned to the infantry. Your mission is to help the South Koreans stop the North Korean advance. At the start of the war, the North Koreans quickly captured Seoul, the South Korean capital. Then they pushed south. The U.S. tanks weren't powerful enough to stop the Soviet-made T-34 tanks the North Koreans have. The U.S. antitank rocket launchers, called bazookas, also weren't effective against the T-34s.

Harry's staying in California for more training. You say good-bye as the Marine brigade prepares to sail to Korea. The brigade is equipped with new, more powerful tanks and M20 bazookas. When you arrive you quickly join the counterattack against the communists.

On the battlefield tanks from both sides rumble forward, firing large guns. Your job is to load 9-pound rockets into a bazooka, which your partner, Roger, fires at the target. U.S. warplanes roar overhead, attacking North Korean infantry. The temperature hits 100 degrees, and you start to feel weak. But you push on.

You and Roger spot several T-34s to the west. You quickly load the bazooka and Roger fires. "It's a hit!" you yell.

American soldiers are ready to fire a bazooka.

Turn the page.

U.S. tanks also fire at the T-34s. One scores a hit. The other North Korean tanks turn to flee. But one fires a last shot at your position. The shell explodes nearby, propelling you and Roger through the air. Pain shoots through your leg. Medics quickly put you and Roger on stretchers and load you into jeeps. You're rushed to an aid station.

At the station you pass out from the pain. You awake a few minutes later to hear a doctor say, "We have to cut it off."

"You have to cut off my leg?" you cry.

64 The doctor nods. You fight back tears. You can't imagine losing part of your leg. But it's better than dying. And it means your stay in Korea will soon be over.

THE END

To follow another path, turn to page 11.
To read the conclusion, turn to page 103.

You tell Rocky, "Cover me if any Chinese pop out."

"You're crazy!" Rocky whispers as you run to the foxhole. You pull the pin from a grenade and fling it into the hole. As it explodes, the sound draws out other Chinese in nearby holes. They begin firing at you. As Rocky fires back, you fling more grenades at the other foxholes. You hear firing from a Chinese weapon the Marines call a burp gun. The guns got the name because of the sound they make. You draw your pistol and fire, killing several more enemy troops. Finally everything is quiet.

65

Rocky runs over to you. "You'll probably get a medal," Rocky says. "You must have killed a dozen of them!"

Turn the page.

"All I want is to get home in one piece." But as you say that, you notice blood trickling from your upper arm. You hope you find UN medics nearby to treat your wound.

THE END

To follow another path, turn to page 11.
To read the conclusion, turn to page 103.

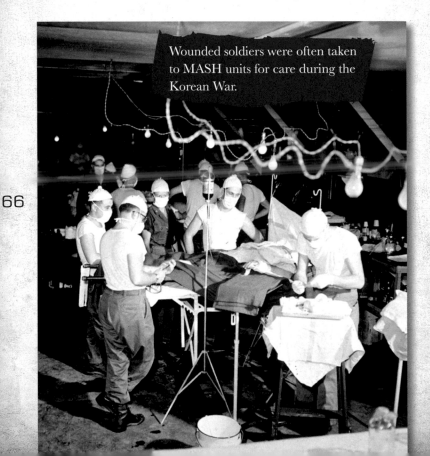

Wounded soldiers were often taken to MASH units for care during the Korean War.

Rocky's right. The two of you could be greatly outnumbered. You move around the edge of the foxhole. But Rocky trips on a rock near another hole. As he falls the noise of his gun hitting the ground stirs the Chinese soldiers nearby. Several bullets rip into you, killing you before you can even raise your gun.

THE END

To follow another path, turn to page 11.
To read the conclusion, turn to page 103.

You jump out of the foxhole and run, joining other Marines trying to escape the Chinese troops. U.S. artillery begins to hit the Chinese. After about 15 minutes of running, you find another Marine unit on a hillside. The troops have taken cover while the artillery shells bombard the enemy. The fighting stops just before dawn.

After a few hours of sleep, you awake with a stabbing pain in your stomach. You try to eat breakfast, but you vomit your food. A medic comes over to treat you.

"I'm not sure what it is," he says. "Maybe a stomach virus."

But you quickly grow weaker. The medic sends you to an aid station several miles from the fighting. A doctor there examines you.

"You might have a parasite in your intestines," he says. "You need treatment right away, or you could die." A helicopter takes you to a hospital. You don't know if you'll ever return to the fighting. All you care about is getting well.

THE END

To follow another path, turn to page 11.
To read the conclusion, turn to page 103.

South Korean soldiers take target practice during their training.

CHAPTER 4

Fighting for Your Homeland

You live in a small village near Pusan, one of South Korea's major ports. Not far away are islands that belong to Japan.

Your family, like many Koreans, suffered under Japanese rule. Your uncle died during a rebellion in 1919. The Japanese killed several thousand Koreans at that time. To the Japanese, Koreans were no better than slaves.

71

You were a boy when Japan attacked the United States in 1941, as part of World War II. Your parents hoped the Americans would drive the Japanese out of Korea. When that finally happened in 1945, your whole village celebrated.

Turn the page.

But since 1948 your new country of South Korea has faced another danger. The communists in the north want to control all of Korea. You and your friends discuss whether the communists might start a war.

"Kim Il Sung is crazy," your friend Dae says. "He wants to invade us."

"But the Americans can stop him," you say.

"That's not what Mr. Pak thinks," Dae says. Mr. Pak once studied in Pusan and is considered the smartest man in town. "He says the communists could take over before the United States could respond."

"That's because our military is so weak," says another friend, Jin. "The weapons we have are old or broken."

"Maybe the Americans will give us better weapons," Dae says. "But until then our country needs more soldiers. I'm going to volunteer for the Republic of Korea Army." Dae looks at you and Jin. "Will you come with me?"

You would like to fight for your country. But your father needs your help on his fishing boat. Selling fish is the only way the family makes money.

Jin says, "I will." He looks at you. "What about you?"

To volunteer for the army, turn to page **74**.

To stay home, turn to page **79**.

The three of you go to Pusan to enlist. The sergeant is surprised to see volunteers. "Usually we have to pull guys off the street to get new soldiers," he says. You all head off for training.

Only there's not much of it. Jin was right. The ROK Army is in bad shape. But American soldiers have trained some of the officers. Others fought with the Chinese against the Japanese during World War II. You learn basic skills, such as how to fire a rifle and a mortar.

Late in 1949 you and Dae are assigned to an army division near the city of Kaesong, north of the 38th parallel. Jin remains in the south. The border between the two Koreas stretches about 150 miles. You realize that the ROK Army doesn't have enough troops to defend it well.

Turn to page 76.

A group of U.S. Marines arrives in Pusan, South Korea, ready to fight. Pusan was part of a small area that remained in South Korean hands after the North Korean invasion.

The morning of June 25, 1950, the sound of artillery jerks you awake. The North Koreans are attacking! It's Sunday, and many soldiers have been given permission to go home for the weekend. You and the others still at the base spring into action.

The North Koreans have more soldiers than the south does. And they have a very effective weapon—Soviet T-34 tanks. You see other ROK soldiers using bazookas to launch rockets at the tanks. The shells just bounce off the tanks' metal armor. As troops realize they can't stop the enemy tanks, many begin to run away. The ROK has no tanks or planes for defense.

Dae starts running away. "Come on!" he yells.

"Don't just stand there," a soldier named Paik says. "Help us!"

To stay and fight with Paik, go to page **77**.

To run with Dae, turn to page **87**.

Paik and several other soldiers grab grenades from the bodies of dead soldiers. Other soldiers come forward with explosives used to blow up bridges and buildings. Paik hands you some grenades. "We're going to charge the enemy tanks and blow them up," he says.

You step back in horror. "You're going to kill yourself to destroy a tank?"

Paik nods. "We have to slow the North Koreans. Maybe the army will be able to send reinforcements if we hold them off."

You hear an explosion nearby. The first of the suicide teams has attacked a T-34 tank. The blast leaves the tank mangled. There's no sign of the bodies of the South Koreans who attacked it.

77

Turn the page.

Another team of soldiers runs toward a T-34.
Enemy machine guns cut them down.

"Are you ready?" Paik asks.

To attack the tank, turn to page **89**.

To stay behind, turn to page **91**.

South Korean troops march
to the front lines.

During the next year, you work on your father's small boat. You also hear from Mr. Pak about skirmishes along the 38th parallel.

"We will be at war again soon," he warns. "You might have to fight after all."

Sure enough, North Korea invades your country in June. The newspapers from Pusan report the war isn't going well for South Korea.

In August you go to Pusan with your father to sell fish. On the street you see soldiers yelling at young men. One soldier sees you and comes over.

"We need soldiers," he says. "Come with me." He grabs your arm and pulls you toward a truck. You yell for your father, but he can't hear you over the noises in the street.

Turn the page.

The truck takes you to an army base. Before you know it, you're boarding a large ship.

South Korea is sending you to Japan to receive training from the U.S. Army. You spend a month there before returning to Korea with the U.S. troops. You learn a few words of English, but mostly you are confused and homesick.

Each Korean soldier is teamed with an American soldier. Your partner is Joe. You use gestures to communicate. You don't always understand Joe, but you like him.

In November your unit is sent to Wonsan, North Korea. The fighting has shifted above the 38th parallel after the Americans helped lead a counterattack. A Korean officer explains you have a choice in the fighting to come. You can work as a scout or be a laborer who helps carry supplies and the wounded.

As a scout you'll be dangerously close to the enemy. But you'd like to show Joe and the Americans that you're as brave as they are.

To be a scout, turn to page **82**.

To be a laborer, turn to page **95**.

U.S. Marines advance toward enemy troops after a successful air strike.

Fighting is heavy near Chosin Reservoir. The Chinese surround a number of Marines there. Your unit is just one of many that will try to help them get out. The Chinese will have to send some of their troops to attack you and other reinforcements. That will keep them from blocking the Marines' main escape route.

You and several other Korean soldiers get orders to scout the nearby hills. The weather has turned bitterly cold. You carry an M1 rifle, the same gun most American troops use. As you inch across the rocky countryside, you hear a noise ahead. You motion for the others to stop.

"What is it?" says another scout, Choo.

"I don't know," you say. "Maybe the Chinese. Or maybe just an animal."

"We should go back," Choo says. You know it's a scout's job to investigate. But if you run into Chinese soldiers, you may never be able to report what you found.

To go back, turn to page **84**.

To go forward, turn to page **85**.

U.S. Marines hike up mountain roads to reach Chosin Reservoir.

You return to the base and report that you heard something, but you weren't sure if it was the enemy. The American officers call in a reconnaissance plane to check out the location. The pilot saw no Chinese in the area. You feel like a coward for turning back.

Enemy troops might not have been where you scouted, but they are close by. That night Chinese artillery shells pelt the camp. Waves of Chinese infantry pour out of the hills. You jump into a nearby foxhole. Before Joe can reach one of the holes, you hear him scream. He's been hit! He falls to the ground.

84

Your first thought is to help Joe. But with so many Chinese around, you could die before you reach him.

To help Joe, turn to page **98**.

To stay in the foxhole, turn to page **99**.

"We're scouts," you say. "We have to see what's up ahead."

You move forward. From behind some rocks, about a dozen Chinese soldiers pop up. Their guns are aimed at you. If you reach for your M1, they'll kill you.

"Come with us," one of the Chinese says in Korean. The Chinese take you to their camp, where other prisoners of war are held. They include Americans and Koreans. That night you begin to march. You march for several weeks, mostly at night, with almost no food.

Finally you reach a prisoner of war camp somewhere in North Korea. You have no sense of how far you've walked or where you are.

Turn the page.

The Chinese hold classes to teach you about Communism. They try to explain why Korea will be better under a united communist government. Choo and several other prisoners decide they will fight for the communists. A Chinese officer asks if you will join them.

To refuse, turn to page **100**.

To agree, turn to page **101**.

North Korean and Chinese forces celebrate a victorious battle.

Dae's running south, away from the 38th parallel. You join him. Shells from enemy tanks and artillery explode all around you.

As you run you wonder if the army will arrest you for desertion. You might be safer if you can blend in with a group of civilians. You and Dae peel off your military uniforms, keeping only your T-shirts and pants. You join a large group of refugees fleeing the advancing North Koreans.

That night you and Dae find a spot off the road to sleep. You reach the capital city of Seoul early the next day. People there are panicking. Thousands of North Korean troops are heading 87 for Seoul. You find an empty building where you can stay the night.

Dae wakes you around midnight. "Everyone is leaving the city. We should too."

Turn the page.

You get up and join the crowd fleeing the city. After about two hours you reach a bridge across the Han River. You'll keep moving south to your village. But with your next step, the bridge explodes. The ROK Army planted explosives to blow up the bridge so the North Koreans couldn't use it. But the order to set off the explosives came too soon. You, Dae, and hundreds of others die in the blast.

THE END

To follow another path, turn to page 11.
To read the conclusion, turn to page 103.

You hold the grenades and wait for Paik to give the signal. "Now!"

You, Paik, and two other soldiers charge the nearest tank. As you run you feel something pierce your left leg—you've been hit! You tumble to the ground as pain shoots through your body.

Meanwhile, Paik and the others run toward the enemy tank and climb on top of it. The tank's turret spins as the soldiers inside try to force off the South Koreans. Then Paik and the others pull their grenade pins. When the smoke clears, you can see the tank is damaged. There's no sign of your fellow soldiers.

89

Turn the page.

The North Koreans are closing in around you. You bury yourself into the ground, trying to play dead. One North Korean comes over and kicks you. You fight back a scream and stay motionless. He walks past.

After several hours the battlefield is mostly quiet. The enemy has wiped out your company and moved south. You try to ignore the moans of dying men as you crawl away. Your wound has stopped bleeding, but it hurts to walk. You look for a farmhouse or a village—somewhere that you can get water and rest. You only hope the North Koreans won't capture or kill you before you find help.

THE END

To follow another path, turn to page 11.
To read the conclusion, turn to page 103.

As Paik gives the order to charge, you stay behind. The men run toward a tank. They climb onto it, and then set off their grenades. The attack worked! The tank is a burning heap of metal. But Paik and the others are dead.

"Retreat!" an officer nearby yells. You and other ROK troops run, while others drive away in trucks and jeeps supplied by the Americans.

Over the next several months, the North Koreans continue to advance. They capture the capital city of Seoul and seem about to seize the whole country. But ROK and U.S. forces pull back to a small corner of South Korea near Pusan. They hold off the enemy as troops and weapons from the United States and other countries reach South Korea.

91

Turn the page.

The Americans launch a major assault on the port city of Inchon on September 15. Your company is now working with U.S. troops, and you've been advancing north from Pusan. You cross the Han River into Seoul on September 25.

The North Koreans are dug in, but some U.S. victories have weakened them. You advance toward 860-foot-high Namsan, which the Americans call South Mountain. It's the highest point in Seoul. In a nighttime attack, your company fires on a smaller hill nearby. Suddenly an enemy shell lands to your left. The explosion knocks you hard on your back. You try to move, but pain shoots down your legs.

A medic runs to your side. "You might have broken your back," he says. "We have to get you to the hospital."

The successful U.S. and South Korean capture of Inchon, South Korea, was a turning point in the war.

93

Turn the page.

The fighting goes on all night. The next day in the hospital, you hear some good news. Your company took the hill, and Namsan is under U.S. control. Almost all North Koreans have fled the city. The war isn't over, but you're glad you helped free Seoul from the enemy.

THE END

To follow another path, turn to page 11.
To read the conclusion, turn to page 103.

U.S. soldiers receive medical treatment at a first aid station.

You'll help with supplies. Many South Korean soldiers do the same work so the more-skilled American soldiers can fight. The Chinese are now helping the North Koreans. In many battles they greatly outnumber the U.S. forces.

Turn the page.

U.S. Marines and Army troops are doing the main fighting in your area. Your unit mostly patrols the region. At times you carry bullets for the U.S. troops' rifles.

Late in November the Americans celebrate a holiday they call Thanksgiving. You eat a bird called turkey for the first time. It tastes good.

But soon the fighting begins again. The Chinese attack in huge numbers. After one battle you help carry litters holding wounded soldiers. You pick up the end of one litter and see that the wounded soldier is Joe! You fight back tears as you carry your friend to the medical station.

You carry many wounded men that day. Some die before the doctors can help them. Later you learn that Joe was sent to a hospital back in South Korea.

As the months drag on, more American troops reach Korea. They replace Koreans in your unit. One day you receive good news. You can go home. As a truck drives you toward Pusan, you pass villages destroyed by the fighting. But the fighting never reached your village. When you get there, you see your father. He welcomes you home with a big hug.

THE END

To follow another path, turn to page 11.
To read the conclusion, turn to page 103.

You jump out of the foxhole and run to Joe. He's bleeding from the stomach, but his eyes are open.

You drag Joe to the nearest foxhole. You manage to get him inside. The Chinese are still moving forward, but overhead you hear the sound of airplanes. It's the Marines in their Corsairs! The planes begin firing rockets and dropping bombs filled with napalm. You peek out and see many of the Chinese burning from the chemical. Others are turning back. The counterattack is a success. But as you look at Joe, you see his eyes are closed. You put your ear to his chest—his breathing has stopped. You hope you never have to see another friend die like this.

THE END

To follow another path, turn to page 11.
To read the conclusion, turn to page 103.

The Chinese are advancing toward your foxhole. One of them stabs Joe with his bayonet, killing him. You stand in the foxhole and fire your gun. Several enemy soldiers fall. You reach for a grenade to try to kill more, but three Chinese jump into the foxhole. Before you can defend yourself, you feel the cold steel of bayonets piercing your body. Within seconds, you're dead.

99

To follow another path, turn to page 11.
To read the conclusion, turn to page 103.

"I won't fight," you say. You remember Joe. "The Americans are good to us. And they want us to be free."

Two Chinese soldiers drag you away and begin beating you. You might not survive, but at least you spoke the truth about how you feel.

100

THE END

To follow another path, turn to page 11.
To read the conclusion, turn to page 103.

You love your homeland, but you want to live. You agree to fight for the Chinese.

You quickly learn that Communism is not as great as the Chinese say. China has many soldiers, but it lacks supplies. During the times when you fight the Americans, you receive food. But when the fighting ends, you go several days without food. When the weather turns cold, your hands turn white with frostbite. Disease spreads through your camp.

One night you sneak away from the camp. You hope you can find American troops. With the English you know, you can convince them to help you. Whatever happens, you'd rather take your chances on your own than fight for the communists.

101

THE END

To follow another path, turn to page 11.
To read the conclusion, turn to page 103.

WELCOME 환영
GATE TO FREEDOM
자유 의 문 으로

Opposing sides of the Korean War traded
prisoners after the fighting ended.

CHAPTER 5

Lasting Tensions

The first year of the Korean War saw the two sides exchange control of large parts of the Korean peninsula. But starting in mid-1951, most of the fighting took place not far from the 38th parallel. That year the two sides also began to discuss how to end the war. But the fighting dragged on until July 27, 1953, when North and South Korea signed an armistice agreement.

The Korean War claimed many lives. About 44,000 Americans died or were reported missing during the war. More than 217,000 South Koreans were killed or missing. The Chinese and North Koreans had more than 1 million men killed or missing.

103

The war ended with Korea still split into two countries. Separating them is a strip of land about 2.5 miles wide and 155 miles long. It's called the demilitarized zone (DMZ). Neither country can place weapons in the zone. But both sides keep troops just outside it.

After the war communists remained in power in the north. Kim Il Sung cut off the country from most of the rest of the world. The Communist Party tightly controlled the government, and the people couldn't elect their leaders. At times the country also struggled to feed its own people, because Kim spent much of the country's money on its military. The conditions continued after Kim's death, when his son Kim Jong Il came to power. In 2011 Kim Jong Il died. His son Kim Jong Un became North Korea's leader.

South Korea remained friendly with the United States. For many years, though, the government limited democracy. Free presidential elections were held for the first time in 1987. Beginning in the 1960s, South Korea created a strong economy. Its companies built cars and electronic devices sold around the world.

After the war tensions remained high between the north and south. Because there was no peace treaty, North Korea says the war is still going on. At times North Korea has launched small military attacks. At other times its leaders have offered to hold talks to improve relations with both South Korea and the United States. North Korea has also threatened to launch nuclear weapons against other nations, including the United States. Some world leaders still worry about another war someday erupting on the Korean peninsula.

TIMELINE

1910—Korea comes under Japanese control.

1919—Thousands of Koreans are killed during the March Uprising against the Japanese.

1945—After World War II, the Soviets control North Korea, and U.S. troops control South Korea.

1948—Syngman Rhee is elected president of Korea. Communists in the north reject his victory and form their own government. North and South Korea are split along the 38th parallel.

1950

June 25—North Korea invades the south; the United States and other nations send troops to help the South Koreans.

June 28—About 800 Koreans fleeing Seoul are killed when the ROK Army deploys a bomb on the Hangang Bridge without warning.

September 15–19—U.S. forces lead an amphibious invasion at Inchon.

October—China enters the war to support North Korea.

November 27—Chinese troops attack UN troops at Chosin Reservoir in North Korea.

December 6–11—U.S. Marines and Army troops pull out of the Chosin Reservoir after causing major Chinese casualties.

December 26—General Matthew Ridgway takes command of the 8th U.S. Army.

1951

January 25—U.S. forces launch a counterattack against the Chinese.

April 11—President Harry Truman relieves General Douglas MacArthur of Allied command in Korea. General Matthew Ridgway replaces MacArthur.

June 19—President Truman signs a law extending the military draft to July 1955 and lowering the draft age to 18.

July 10—Armistice talks begin, but fighting continues.

1952

May 12—General Mark Clark replaces General Ridgway as commander of UN forces in Korea.

August 29—More than 1,400 UN planes bomb Pyongyang, North Korea, in the largest air raid of the war.

November 4—Dwight D. Eisenhower is elected president of the United States.

December 5–8—Eisenhower visits Korea.

1953

April 20–26—In Operation Little Switch, sick and wounded prisoners of war on both sides are exchanged.

July 27—The two sides agree to an armistice, but not a peace treaty.

August 5–September 6—The last POWs on both sides are released.

OTHER PATHS
TO EXPLORE

In this book you've seen how events surrounding the Korean War look different from several points of view. Perspectives on history are as varied as the people who lived it. Seeing history from many points of view is an important part of understanding it.

Here are ideas for other points of view to explore:

You are an American nurse who volunteers to serve in South Korea. How are conditions different from the hospitals in the United States? What's it like being one of the few women in a war zone? (Common Core: Integration of Knowledge and Ideas)

You are an African-American soldier in the U.S. Army. In 1948 President Harry Truman ordered the desegregation of the military. In Korea black and white soldiers serve together in the same units. What is it like living and working closely with whites for the first time? (Common Core: Integration of Knowledge and Ideas)

You are a North Korean. You welcomed the end of Japan's rule, but you dislike Kim Il Sung's tight control over the government. Which government would you rather live under? (Common Core: Integration of Knowledge and Ideas)

READ MORE

Corrigan, Jim. *The Korean War.* Greensboro, N.C.: Morgan Reynolds Pub., 2013.

Jeffrey, Gary. *The Korean War.* New York: Crabtree Publishing Company, 2014.

Raum, Elizabeth. *North Korea.* Chicago: Heinemann Library, 2012.

INTERNET SITES

Use FactHound to find Internet sites related to this book. All of the sites on FactHound have been researched by our staff.

Here's all you do:
Visit *www.facthound.com*
Type in this code: 9781491403556

GLOSSARY

amphibious attack (am-FI-bee-uhs uh-TAK)—a military action involving forces landing and attacking from the sea

armistice (ARM-iss-tiss)—a formal agreement to stop fighting

artillery (ar-TIL-uh-ree)—cannons and other large guns used during battles

bazooka (buh-ZOO-kuh)—a shoulder-held weapon that fires small, explosive rockets

Communism (KAHM-yuh-ni-zuhm)—a form of government that limits personal freedom and the right to own property

infantry (IN-fuhn-tree)—soldiers who fight on foot

latitude (LAT-uh-tood)—the position of a place in degrees north or south of the equator

litter (LIT-ur)—a lightweight stretcher for carrying a sick or wounded person

mortar (MOR-tur)—a small, portable weapon that fires shells or rockets

napalm (NAY-pahm)—a highly flammable chemical

reconnaissance (ree-KAH-nuh-suhnss)—a mission to gather information about an enemy

BIBLIOGRAPHY

Alexander, Bevin. *Korea: The First War We Lost.* New York: Hippocrene Books, 2000.

Carlson, Lewis H. *Remembered Prisoners of a Forgotten War: An Oral History of the Korean War POWs.* New York: St. Martin's Press, 2002.

Condon, John P. *Corsairs to Panthers: U.S. Marine Aviation in Korea.* Washington, D.C.: U.S. Marine Corps Historical Center, 2002.

Halberstam, David. *The Coldest Winter: America and the Korean War.* New York: Hyperion, 2007.

Halliday, Jon, and Bruce Cumings. *Korea: The Unknown War.* New York: Pantheon Books, 1988.

McManus, John C. *The 7th Infantry Regiment: Combat in an Age of Terror: The Korean War Through the Present.* New York: Forge, 2008.

O'Donnell, Patrick K. *Give Me Tomorrow: The Korean War's Greatest Untold Story—The Epic Stand of the Marines of George Company.* Cambridge, Mass.: Da Capo Press, 2010.

Paik Sun Yup. *From Pusan to Panmunjom.* Washington, D.C.: Brassey's, 1992.

Richardson, William, and Kevin Maurer. *Valleys of Death: A Memoir of the Korean War.* New York: Berkley Caliber, 2010.

Russ, Martin. *Breakout: The Chosin Reservoir Campaign, Korea 1950.* New York: Fromm International, 1999.

Summers, Harry G., Jr. *Korean War Almanac.* New York: Facts on File, 1990.

INDEX